Air Stewardess.

Titles in the series

The Air Stewardess   0 241 11209 5
The Dustman   0 241 11210 9
The Farmer   0 241 10937 X
The Fireman   0 241 10936 1
The Hairdresser   0 241 11211 7
The Lorry Driver   0 241 11164 1
The Milkman   0 241 10934 5
The Nurse   0 241 11162 5
The Policewoman   0 241 10935 3
The Postman   0 241 11163 3
The Vet   0 241 11165 X
The Zoo-keeper   0 241 11212 5

The author and publishers would like to thank
Sally Enoch and British Airways for their help and
co-operation in the production of this book.

Layout by Andrew Shoolbred

First published in Great Britain 1984 by
Hamish Hamilton Children's Books
Garden House, 57–59 Long Acre, London WC2E 9JZ
Copyright © 1984 by Hamish Hamilton

British Library Cataloguing in Publication Data
Stewart, Anne
The air stewardess. – (Cherrystones series)
1. Air lines – Flight attendants
Juvenile literature
I. Title II. Fairclough, Chris
III. Series
387.7'42 HD6073.A43

ISBN 0-241-11209-5

Printed in Great Britain by
Cambus Litho Ltd East Kilbride Scotland

CHERRYSTONES

The Air Stewardess

Anne Stewart

Photographs by
Chris Fairclough

Hamish Hamilton · London

S187076 629.136

Sally Enoch is an air stewardess. She works for British Airways and travels all over the world. Some trips take three weeks, others only a couple of days.

Today, Sally is flying to New York. She will only be away one night, but she packs three different outfits – a summer dress, a winter dress, and a pair of jeans and blouse. She can never be sure what the weather will be like in another country. Sally's dog, Benson, watches her. He looks as if he would like to go too.

It takes Sally about ten minutes to drive to the airport.
She lives nearby because when crew are on stand-by, they
often have to get there in a hurry. But most of the time
they are given their timetables at least one month in
advance. They know exactly which flights they will be on.

When Sally gets to the airport, she drives to Tristar House. This is where BA cabin crew report for work. She loads her case on to a special conveyor belt and makes sure the yellow label is tied on securely. The label shows baggage handlers that the case belongs to one of the crew.

After Sally has parked her car, she goes inside and signs the crew list to show she has arrived. If the crew is not complete one and a quarter hours before take-off, someone on stand-by has to be called out to take the missing person's place. There are thirteen crew on this Boeing 747 flight.

About an hour before take-off, the Cabin Service Officer (CSO) holds a meeting for the crew. This is called a briefing. First he introduces himself and the two pursers, his next in command. He tells them how many First Class, Super Club and Tourist passengers there are, and whether there is anybody who will need special attention. He asks if anyone can speak a foreign language or has nursing experience.

Sally then fetches the cash box. The girl behind the counter hands her some English and American money and Sally signs to say she will be responsible for it. When passengers pay for drinks or duty-free goods during the flight, Sally locks the money away in the cash box. On her return to London, she pays the money in to the cashiers.

Sally joins the rest of the crew, who are already waiting for their coach to take them to the aircraft. Their luggage has been loaded on to the coach.

By the time the first passengers board, the crew have
checked that the cabins are tidy and that the meals and
drinks have been loaded. Sally checks the passengers'
boarding cards and directs them to their seats.

This aeroplane is a Jumbo jet and can hold nearly 400 people. Today, it is almost full. Most people have Tourist tickets, which are the cheapest. These people board first and sit towards the rear of the plane. In front of them sit Super Club passengers. They are often business-travellers. First Class ticket holders sit at the front.

After about 20 minutes nearly everyone is seated and ready for take-off.

As the plane waits on the runway, the cabin crew show the passengers what to do if there is an emergency. Although emergencies are very rare, this is done before every flight. Here you can see Sally explaining how to put on a life-jacket.

Then she and the other crew check that all the passengers have put their seats into the upright position and have fastened their seat belts. They also make sure that all hand baggage has been safely stowed under the seats or in the overhead lockers.

Just before take-off, the cabin crew pull down special fold-away seats and fasten their own seat belts.

As soon as the plane is airborne, Sally gets up to prepare a cot for a passenger's baby to sleep in during the flight. This is a special BA cot which is packed flat when not needed. When unpacked, it is simply unfolded to make a full-sized cot. After use, it is sterilised and wrapped in cellophane until needed again.

Some older people need special care, too. This elderly
gentleman is feeling cold, so Sally fetches him an airline
blanket and tucks it round his knees. They chat about
his grand-children who live in New Jersey.

'You must be looking forward to seeing them,' says
Sally.

13

It is soon time to serve drinks. A special drinks trolley is wheeled down the aisles, with one steward or stewardess at each end. Inside, there are small cans of soft drinks, miniature bottles of spirits, and stacks of plastic glasses. On an aeroplane, it is vital that everything takes up as little room as possible. And everything must be lightweight.

The cabin crew work very fast and soon everyone has something to drink.

But these two children are getting bored. They are too young to read, there is nowhere to play and nothing to see out of the window. Sally notices them and asks if they would like to do some drawing. She brings them some crayons and colouring books. They decide to start on a picture of a jet.

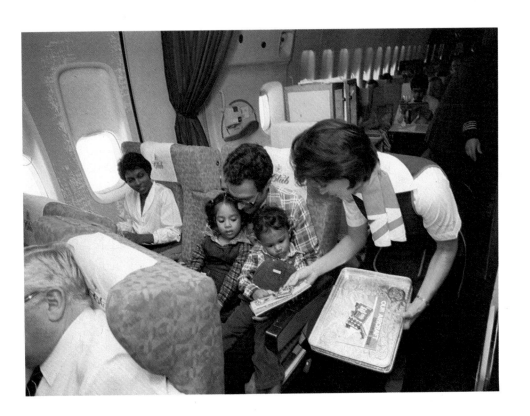

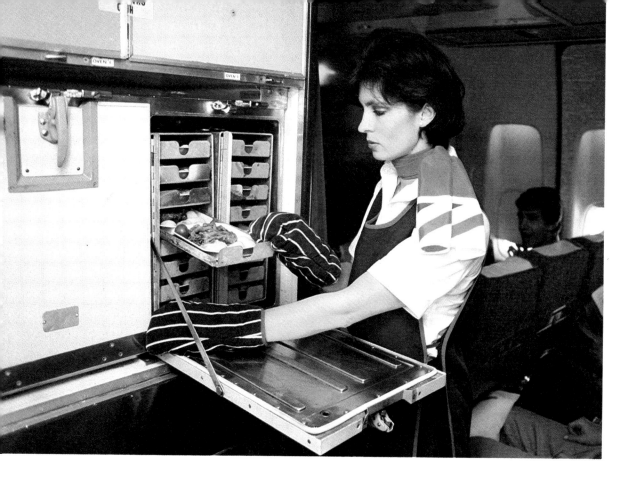

While the glasses are being cleared away, Sally checks that lunch is ready. The oven trays are so hot, she has to wear heat-proof gloves.

Aircraft meals are prepared by BA chefs in a large kitchen at the airport. Here they are partly cooked, and divided into portions. Then they are loaded on to the aeroplane. All the cabin crew have to do is heat them up.

Today, the main course in Super Club is a choice of steak or duck. Passengers in First Class are offered a different menu with a much wider choice of dishes. Passengers in any class who may not eat certain foods can order a special meal when booking their ticket.

After lunch, Sally and Alan set up a display of duty-free goods for passengers to buy. Alan is one of many stewards working for British Airways.

There are bottles of whisky, gin and other spirits, perfume and cigarettes, as well as a few small gifts. Normally, a shop has to charge tax (or duty) on these things, but on an aeroplane flight the airline can sell them duty-free. This means they are much cheaper than usual. These two ladies are buying perfume to give to their daughters at home. Sally works out how much the price is in dollars.

The film comes next. On a 747, three different films are
shown at the same time – and to make sure everyone has
a good view, each film is shown on two separate screens.
Here, Sally helps the CSO to uncover one of the screens.
The purser asks the passengers to pull down their window
blinds and the lights go out.

While the passengers are watching the film or having a nap, Sally and the rest of the cabin crew take turns to eat some lunch and snatch a few moments' rest. It is the first time any of them has sat down for nearly five hours. They sit in seats curtained off from the rest of the plane.

But when there are nearly 400 passengers, no-one can relax for long. There is always someone who wants a drink, a cushion, or simply some information. If one part of the plane is busier than another, cabin crew can use an internal telephone to ask for help. In an aircraft as large as this, telephones save both time and energy.

One young passenger, Scott, asks to see the flight deck.
The captain gives his permission and Sally leads Scott up
a short spiral staircase, through a door marked 'Private',
and on to the flight deck. It is very small, measuring only
3 metres square. Captain Shrosbree explains that it has
been specially designed to allow the three-man flight crew
to reach all the knobs and dials with ease. Then he shows
Scott where the plane is on the map.

About 20 minutes later, the plane begins its descent to John F. Kennedy airport, New York. Sally gives out immigration forms to everyone who is not an American citizen. These have to be filled out and given to airport officials after landing. Captain Shrosbree reminds passengers that they should change their watches to American time, which is five hours behind British time.

'It's 1.15 in New York,' he says. 'You're just in time for lunch!'

A couple of hours later Sally is in Manhattan. Although tired after the seven and a half hour flight, she decides to go to Central Park for some fresh air. A policeman points her in the right direction.

'What wouldn't I give to travel round the world, like you,' he says.

'It is fun,' admits Sally, 'and I have visited some marvellous places. But you have to be fit, hard-working, and very patient to take the pace. All the same, I can't imagine doing anything else.'

Index